The Offspring

A Dream **in the Field**

A Poem by Nate Freeman

Illustrated by Jean Cannon

ISBN: 0-9665016-0-8

This book is dedicated to the artists, audience, volunteers, and sponsors who have participated in the annual Manifest Poetry art show staged in Northfield, Vermont since 1995. Many thanks to Dianna Jean (D.J.) Montague for book design and layout. Special thanks also to David Carroll and Kati Dana.

The Offspring: A Dream in the Field, 1997. Tipi, acrylic paint, pine, stain, clay.

Design	Nate Freeman
Visual Artists	Mural by Jean Cannon
	Sculpture by Doug Guy
	Calligraphy by Pamela Brownson
	Clay medallion mold by Andy Hall
Performance Artists	Narration by Nate Freeman
	Percussion by Rob Berman
Direction	Anthony Cosmano

Tipi by Nomadics Tipi Makers
Photography by Glenn Moody Photography
Graphic art design and book layout by Dianna Jean (D.J.) Montague, Holy Cow Graphics
T-shirt design by Mark Lukasiewicz, Bruce Janicke, Hed East

Epigraph from Walt Whitman's *Song of Myself*, song 6, <u>Leaves of Grass</u>

Printed in China

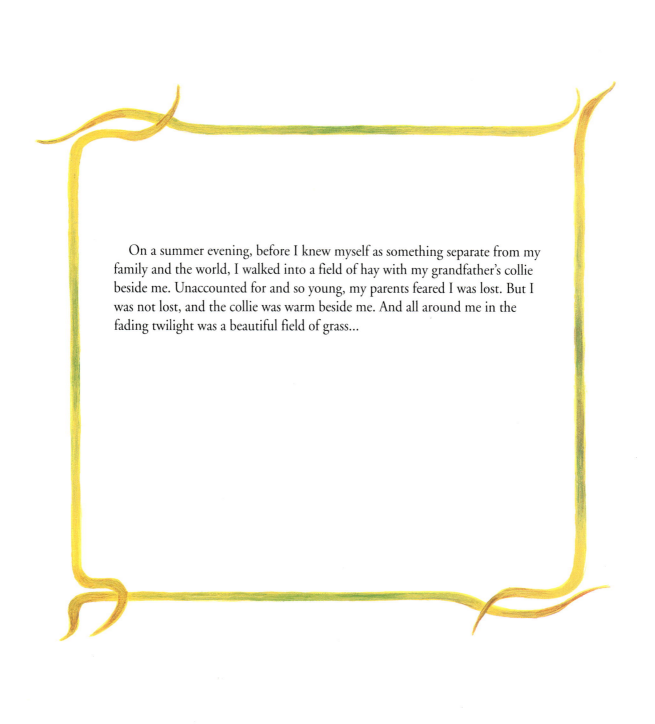

On a summer evening, before I knew myself as something separate from my family and the world, I walked into a field of hay with my grandfather's collie beside me. Unaccounted for and so young, my parents feared I was lost. But I was not lost, and the collie was warm beside me. And all around me in the fading twilight was a beautiful field of grass...

A child said, What is the grass? fetching it to me with full hands;
        How could I answer the child?... I do not know what it is any
    more than he.
I guess it must be the flag of my disposition, out of hopeful green stuff woven.
Or I guess it is the handkerchief of the Lord,
A scented gift and remembrancer designedly dropped.
Bearing its owner's name someway in the corners, that we may see
    and remark, and say Whose?
Or I guess the grass is itself a child...the produced babe of the
    vegetation.

And now it seems to me the beautiful uncut hair of graves.

                                    – Walt Whitman

W hat are you? whispered the tawny grass.
I lowered my ear to its blown kiss
and reached for a leafy beard.

The son of a son of a son, I sang
from the throat of my open palm,
born of a freeman, tied to the land.

Are you the coarse weave of spirits unwound?
Yissssssss...yesssss....
whispered the bracts in the breeze,

we are the sod of your forbears' dreams;
we are the shrill of wind in the trees;
we are morning transparent turning orange to green.

"Tell me, " I spoke, "how I might come to be!
You know the turn and flow of the past;
where will time course for me?"

The air stilled over the autumn grass;
in silence I attended the hay
and lulled into night as the field's shades passed

through blue, dark purple, and gray.
Ten handfuls of stars joined the night sky
and swirled in bright constellation

as I lapsed into dream with cold in my veins
and the dew of my eye
misting the ranked generations.

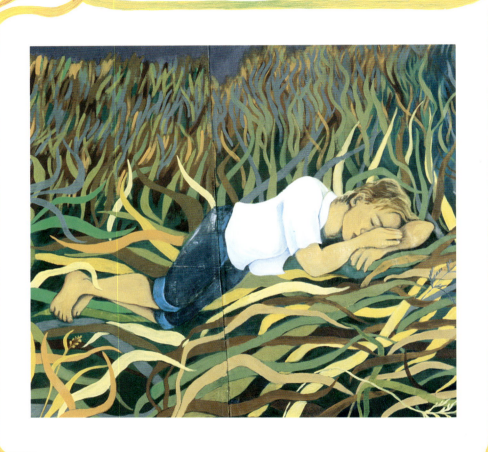

The Changes, the Changes, follow a spiralled string,
twining the colors of ages into a neutral strain,
assuming the probable places of an uncertain chain.

The Changes, the Changes, of our short history lain:
as vast as the western ranges, as swift as remembered pain,
as constant as surf's swelling rages smoothing the landfall's grain.

The Changes, the Changes, ringing like bells in a tower
that summon the grace of angels and sing of the present hour.
They are as gods of mythology's races wearing the day's brightest flower.

The Changes, the Changes, the crossing of hope and doubt,
pitting venerable sages against passion of youth sung loud,
parting our lives into stages of time like steps ascending the round.

The Changes, the Changes, follow a sprialled string,
twining the colors of ages into a neutral strain...

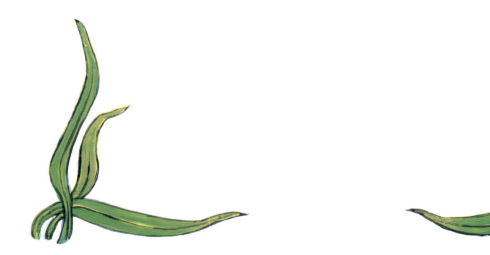

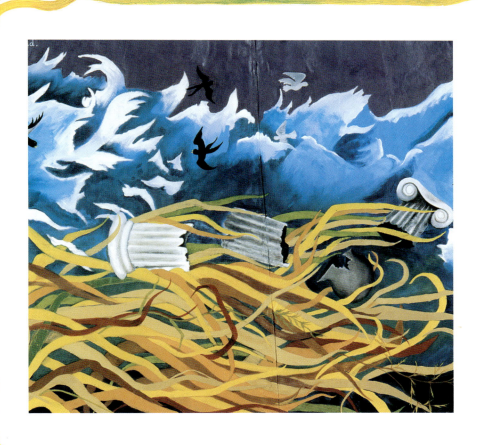

The dream in the grass raised me as though from sleep
to a body now metamorphosed – in form of a native sphinx!

From my back spread the plume of a falcon!
on my frame tawny catamount coat!
from my hind the tail of coyote whipped with life of its own.

What am I? whispered the thoughts of my dream,
How am I turned into beast?
How am I lost in this dark field, and what does all of this mean?

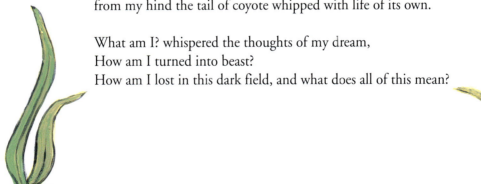

You are the Offspring, the tawny grass sang,
one out of many, born to the land,
raised from the soil and spirits' coarse wend.

Faces appeared in the sweep of the hay
faintly revealing the shimmering shades
as a field of forbears descending each age.

And each of the spirits quietly told
of secrets forgotten from oldest of old
and matters essential for passage and growth.

Wisdom eternal loosed from the field
passing to breezes and whispering lulls:
humility's heroes of earth's timeless hold

breathed from the grass and the sod's weave below...

...And I knew that the life of this land had been hallowed.
And I cried to the faces of past with wolf-howl:

How do we gain these wings
and wander broad over the world to the most lonely realms,
driven as spiritual seekers to mountains, woods, and coasts?

Why do we rarely remember the secrets unveiled for us:
the reasons for fruit and failure passed down from ancestors;
the treasure of former ages, as the clay of poetic genius?

How do we find the field of whispering souls
hidden from searching minds like a mystical world unknown:
above our normal awareness and beneath the course of our goals?

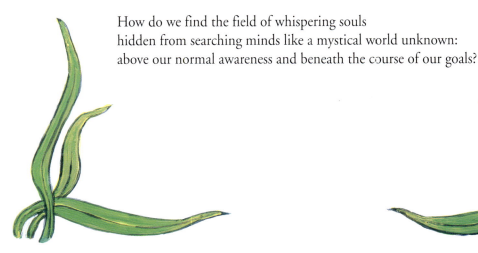

The grass whispered its gentle breeze
waiting to hear the secret in me,
but the Howl, the Howl, shook me from sleep!

I opened my eyes to a luminous moon.
The tawny grass shone like silver spears strewn
over the field in their shadows' dark loom.

But remained in my mind the fantastic scene
of the transfigured beast that inspired my name,
and I sang from the throat of my palm to the breeze:

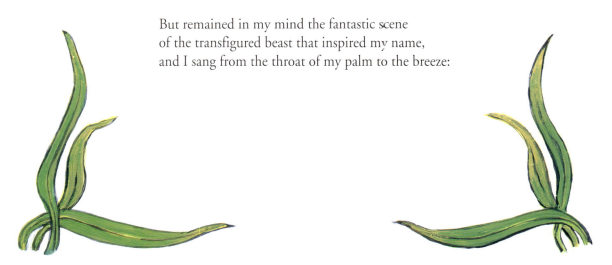

I am the Offspring!
A creature born of a powerful dream!
A native and natural sphinx!

I am a mountain
couching in shape of the lion!
from the stars of the sky I am given wings of the falcon!

Ecstasy! Rapture! Immortal heart!
Raised by the whisper of forebears' words;
raised by the breadth of this fertile earth!

Raised by the weave where I am enthroned
reclaiming the line of old earthly souls
and this sacred sod where the spirits are sown!

I stood from the place where I slept in the field
charged with new knowledge and transcendent zeal,
faithful that history's Changes would lead

off from this moment with heartfelt belief
for the whispering grass and the twine of time's breeze.

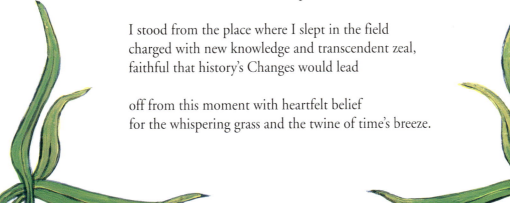

A child said, What is the grass? fetching it to me
with full hands;
How could I answer the child?.... I do not know what it is any more
than he....